# A Guide to
# ROCKS and MINERALS

By Jeffrey Fuerst

Series Literacy Consultant
**Dr Ros Fisher**

PEARSON
Longman

Pearson Education Limited
Edinburgh Gate
Harlow
Essex CM20 2JE
England

www.longman.co.uk

ISBN 0 582 84537 8

Colour reproduction by Colourscan, Singapore
Printed and bound in China by Leo Paper Products Ltd.

The Publisher's policy is to use paper manufactured from sustainable forests.

The following people from **DK** have
contributed to the development of this product:

**Art Director** Rachael Foster

Keith Davis, Carole Oliver **Design** | **Managing Editor** Scarlett O'Hara
Helen McFarland, Pernilla Pearce **Picture Research** | **Editorial** Ben Hoare, Kate Pearce
Richard Czapnik, Andy Smith **Cover Design** | **Production** Rosalind Holmes
Keith Lye **Consultant** | **DTP** David McDonald

**Dorling Kindersley would like to thank:** Rose Horridge in the DK Picture Library, Johnny Pau for additional cover design work.

**Picture Credits:** Corbis: James L. Amos 11br; Craig Aurness 1; Derek Croucher 18bl; Ric Ergenbright 15bl; Jose Fuste Raga 10br; Chinch Gryniewicz/Ecoscene 12; Polak Matthew/Sygma 28bl; Anthony T. Matthews 20br; 21br; Richard Mummins 16br; Roger Ressmeyer 5c, 8b; Scott T. Smith 22br; Lee Snider 19br; Roger Wood 20bl. DK Images: British Museum 26tr. GeoScience Features Picture Library: 18br. Science Photo Library: Gary Hincks 7; Keith Kent 4; Lawrence Lawry 11bcl. Jacket: Corbis: Derek Croucher back.

All other images: DK Dorling Kindersley © 2004. For further information see www.dkimages.com
Dorling Kindersley Ltd., 80 Strand, London WC2R ORL

# Contents

All About Rocks ...................................4

Igneous Rock ...............................7

Sedimentary Rock ........................12

Metamorphic Rock......................17

Minerals.....................................22

A Rock and Mineral Collection ........30

Glossary ....................................31

Index ........................................32

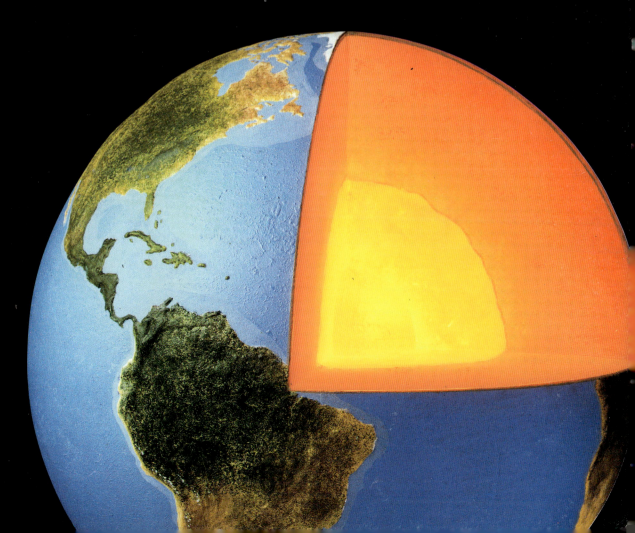

# All About Rocks

From the highest mountain to the deepest ocean floor,
there is rock. Sometimes it is hidden by snow or water.
Other times it is hidden by grass. Rock is everywhere.
This is because the whole of the Earth's **crust** is made
of rock. Rocks are made up of **minerals**.

Above the Earth's surface wind and rain change the
shape of rock. Below the Earth's surface heat and pressure
change the shape of rock.

Rocks give us important clues about the history of the Earth. Scientists who study rocks are called geologists. They study layers of rock to find out the age of the Earth. They also study the changes in the Earth's crust that have taken place over millions of years.

A geologist examines igneous rocks.

gneiss

Geologists have found gneiss rock that they think is 4 billion years old.

# How To Use This Book

This book is a guide to the main types of rocks and some different **minerals**. It is divided into four sections: **igneous rock**, **sedimentary rock**, **metamorphic rock** and minerals. Each section begins with an introduction to the type of rock or mineral. Then there is an explanation of each rock in that category. All the rocks are listed in alphabetical order.

Type of rock or mineral

Name of a rock or mineral in that category

Description of this rock or mineral

IGNEOUS ROCK

fine grains

coarse grains

## Basalt

Basalt is found all over the Earth. It is formed from **lava**. It is dark grey and often has lighter markings across its surface. Basalt is made up of fine **grains**. It is used for building roads.

Giant's Causeway in Northern Ireland is made of basalt.

## Granite

Granite is found in and around mountains. It is formed from **magma**. It is white, grey, pink or yellow and has streaks of different colours. Granite is made up of coarse grains. It is used to make gravestones, paving stones and for building bridges.

Tower Bridge in London is made of granite.

10

# Igneous Rock

The Earth's **crust** is made up mostly of rocks formed from molten material. These rocks are called igneous (ig-NEE-us) rocks. Deep inside the Earth is liquid rock called **magma**. When magma cools and hardens slowly inside the crust, far below the surface, it produces one type of igneous rock.

Some magma reaches the surface through volcanoes. It is called **lava**. When lava cools and hardens on or near the surface, then it produces another type of igneous rock.

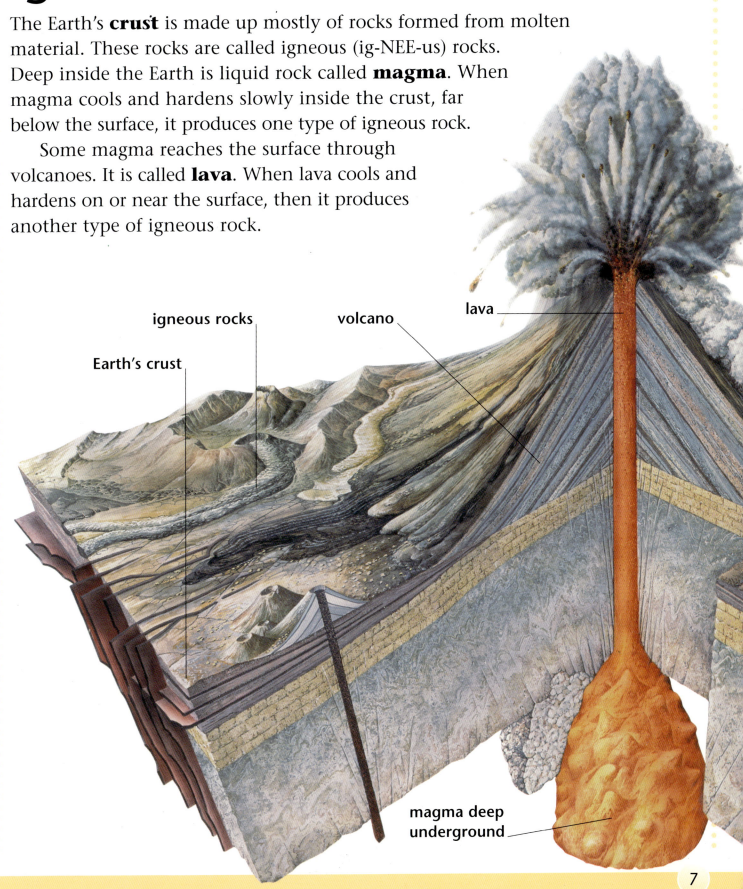

igneous rocks

volcano

lava

Earth's crust

magma deep underground

ropy lava

It is possible to tell where a rock has formed by looking at its **crystals** and **grain** size. **Igneous rock** that forms outside a volcano cools and hardens quickly. There is little time to grow crystals before the rock hardens. Therefore, these rocks have small crystals and fine grains.

Basalt has small crystals and fine grains. It is also formed outside a volcano. It contains the **minerals** olivine, augite and feldspar.

Red-hot liquid rock flows out of a volcano.

Some igneous rock forms inside the Earth's crust where the **magma** hardens slowly. Then there is much more time to grow crystals before the rock hardens. Therefore, these rocks have large crystals and coarse grains.

Granite has large crystals and coarse grains. It is also formed inside a volcano. It contains the minerals quartz, mica and feldspar.

Granite is made up of the minerals feldspar, quartz and mica.

granite

quartz

mica

feldspar

fine grains

# Basalt

Basalt is found all over the Earth. It is formed from **lava**. It is dark grey and often has lighter markings across its surface. Basalt is made up of fine **grains**. It is used for building roads.

coarse grains

# Granite

Granite is found in and around mountains. It is formed from **magma**. It is white, grey, pink or yellow and has streaks of different colours. Granite is made up of coarse grains. It is used to make gravestones, paving stones and for building bridges.

Giant's Causeway in Northern Ireland is made of basalt.

Tower Bridge in London is made of granite.

uncut diamond

coarse grains

very tiny grains

# Kimberlite

Kimberlite is found in the Earth's **crust**. It is formed from magma. It forms tube and bowl shapes. It is dark blue. Kimberlite is made up of coarse grains. It is often made up of other rocks and **minerals** like garnets and diamonds.

# Obsidian

Obsidian is found around volcanoes. It is formed from lava. It is a natural glass. It is black and sometimes has spots or bands of other colours. Obsidian is made up of tiny grains. Thousands of years ago it was used to cut things or for weapons. Today it is used in jewellery.

## Diamonds in Kimberlite

Diamonds are the hardest rocks on Earth. They are very valuable. Natural diamonds don't sparkle. First they are taken from rocks like kimberlite. Then they are cut and polished. This makes them sparkle.

uncut diamond          cut diamond

Obsidian was often used in early tools, such as this dagger.

# Sedimentary Rock

**Sedimentary rock** makes up part of the Earth's **crust**. It is made up of different layers of rock. It forms at the Earth's surface in different ways. Wind and rain break down rock and move it from place to place. Other times rock is carried down rivers and finally settles on the river bed. This is called sediment.

Over time, loose bits of rock gather and settle. Layers and layers pile up and harden to form sedimentary rock.

These sea cliffs in south Wales are made of sandstone. Different layers of sediment appear as bands in the rock.

Sedimentary rock often contains **fossils**. Sometimes dead animals, insects and plants are captured in the remains of rocks. As each layer of rock piles up, the lower rock packs together. The dead animals, insects or plants are trapped between the layers of rock and preserved.

## How a Fossil Forms

These diagrams show one of the ways in which a fossil may form.

1. A fish dies and sinks to the bottom of the sea.

2. The dead fish is buried, and its soft parts rot away.

3. Over millions of years, the mud turns into rock and the bones become a fossil.

4. Earth movements bring the fossil to the surface.

5. The fossil is an almost perfect copy of the fish.

**dragonfly**

**dragonfly fossil**

A dragonfly was preserved as a fossil in rock.

**fern**

**fern fossil**

Ferns are preserved as fossils in rocks.

cube-shaped crystals

pieces of shell

# Halite

Halite is found in dried-up salt lakes and seas. It is usually white. Halite is often made up of coarse **grains** and may be buried under other sedimentary layers. It is also known as rock salt and is used to season food.

# Limestone

Limestone is found in dried-up salt lakes and seas, too. It is usually creamy yellow. Limestone is made up of fine to coarse grains. It is formed in several ways. Sometimes it is formed from existing **minerals**. Other times it is formed from the remains of once-living things, such as sea shells.

Icicle-like stalactites that hang down from the roofs of caves are made of limestone.

**Crystals** of rock salt are ground to make table salt.

salt grinder

Limestone drips in a cave.

Limestone is used to make cement, tiles, as a fertilizer or to build monuments.

fine sand

large quartz pebbles

## Cliffs of Chalk

Along the coast of the English Channel are the white cliffs of Dover. They are made of soft white chalk which is a type of limestone.

Long ago the cliffs were covered with warm, shallow water. Layers of mud, made up of the remains of tiny sea plants and animals, washed up the sides and hardened to form chalk. Then the sea level dropped and the chalky cliffs were revealed. Now the sea is wearing away these soft chalk cliffs.

# Conglomerate

Conglomerates were formed on ancient beaches and river beds. They are made of fine and large grains. The fine grains are worn fragments such as sand and mud. The large grains are pebbles, often made of the hard mineral quartz.

Conglomerates were formed on beaches.

# Sandstone

Sandstone was formed on ancient beaches and in deserts. It is often yellow. Sandstone is made up of tiny **grains**. It is formed from grains of sand that are cemented together with **minerals** in the water. It is used to build monuments and temples.

# Shale

Shale is formed in water. It is usually grey or purple with blue or black stripes. Shale is made up of fine grains. It is often found with layers of sandstone or limestone. It is used to make bricks, tiles and pottery.

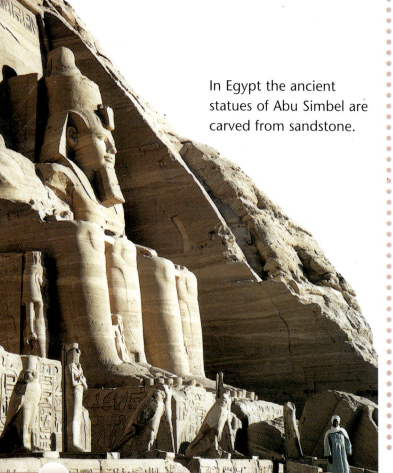

In Egypt the ancient statues of Abu Simbel are carved from sandstone.

Layers of shale and limestone rise up from the sea to form the Moher Cliffs, in Ireland.

# Metamorphic Rocks

**Metamorphic rock** is formed beneath the Earth's surface. Metamorphism means to change form and this describes what has happened to this rock. Metamorphic rock is created when heat or pressure changes a rock into another form.

Different types of heat and pressure change rock into different types of metamorphic rock. Slate is formed at fairly low temperatures and pressures. Quartzite is formed at high temperatures.

## How Grains Change

Usually, a fine grain in a metamorphic rock means that it formed under lower pressure and temperature. Grain size increases with higher temperature and pressure.

**hornfels**

fine grains

**marble**

shale        slate

Intense heat inside the crust changes shale into slate and sandstone into quartzite.

sandstone        quartzite

medium grains

coarse grains

chiastolite hornfels

garnet hornfels

long crystals

# Gneiss

Gneiss (pronounced nice) is commonly found on the Earth's surface. It is often grey or pink. Gneiss is made up of medium to coarse **grains**. It is formed at very high temperatures and pressure. It contains **minerals** including feldspar, mica and quartz.

# Hornfels

Hornfels is a hard, flinty rock. It is often grey or green. Hornfels is made up of fine grains. It is formed near the surface of the Earth at high temperatures and low pressure. There are many different types of hornfels.

Early Scottish people placed these tall gneiss stones in a circle about 3,800 years ago.

Hornfels is a hard, flinty rock. It is usually grey or green.

# Marble

Marble is widely found in the Earth's **crust**. High-grade marble, used in sculpture, is made up of fine or medium grains. It is formed inside the Earth at very high temperatures and pressure. Low-grade marble is coarse-grained.

When limestone is heated it changes into marble. Some minerals inside the limestone produce spots and streaks in the marble. Marble is usually white, grey, green or black.

If marble is polished then its colour and pattern stand out. Marble is used to make sculptures, churches, temples and monuments.

**unpolished marble**

This temple called the Parthenon, is in Athens, Greece, and is made of marble.

Sculptors admire marble for its beauty. It can be carved without splitting.

garnet schist

# Quartzite

Quartzite is another common **metamorphic rock**. It is white, pink or grey. Quartzite is made up of medium to coarse **grains**. It formed at higher temperatures and pressure than most metamorphic rocks. It is used to make road metal and paving blocks to line pavements.

# Schist

Schist is found where mountains have formed. It is usually shiny green or grey and sometimes has glittery specks of colour. Schist is made up of fine to medium grains. It is formed at medium temperatures and pressure.

Quartzite was used for this statue of the Ancient Egyptian god Amun.

Schist rock has been worn away to form this arch on the coast of Scotland.

# Slate

Slate is found around mountains. It is black, blue or grey with tinges of purple, red or green. Slate is made up of fine grains. It is formed from shale at fairly low temperatures and pressure. Different **minerals** in the shale make different types of slate.

All slate splits easily into thin sheets. Many years ago teachers and pupils wrote on sheets of slate with chalk. Today slate is used to make roof or floor tiles and pool table tops.

black slate

green slate

Teachers and pupils wrote on slate with chalk.

chalk

Slate splits easily into thin sheets. This makes it ideal for roof tiles.

# Minerals

Rocks are mixtures of different **minerals**. There are more than 4,000 minerals in the Earth's **crust**, but many of them are rare. The most common minerals are feldspar and quartz.

Many minerals, including **metals** and gemstones, are valuable. People have mined valuable minerals from the rocks for thousands of years. Some minerals are used to make parts for spacecraft, batteries or electric motors. Other minerals are used to make jewellery, vases or bowls.

## Mineral Checklist

Each mineral can be identified by its special features:

- Colour
- Structure: What is the crystal shape or pattern of its grains or **crystals**?
- Hardness: Will it scratch easily?
- Transparency: Does light pass through it?
- Lustre: How does light reflect from its surface?
- Streak: What colour does it leave when it is rubbed across a tile?
- Density: How close together are its **grains**?

quartz

These rock formations in New Mexico are made of quartz.

close-up of quartz crystals

# Testing Mineral Hardness

Minerals are tested for hardness using the Mohs scale. On this scale, any mineral can be compared with ten common minerals that are arranged in order from the softest to the hardest. They are talc, gypsum, calcite, fluorite, apatite, feldspar, quartz, topaz, corundum and diamond. Talc is the softest and diamond is the hardest. Scratching minerals with your fingernail or with a coin gives you some idea of the hardness of softer minerals.

**The Mohs scale**

**10** diamond

**9** corundum

**8** topaz

**7** quartz

**6** feldspar

**5** apatite

**4** fluorite

**3** calcite

**2** gypsum

**1** talc

This scale helps find the hardness of different minerals.

The hardness of some minerals can also be tested with a coin.

# Corundum

Corundum is found mainly in **metamorphic rocks** formed from shale and limestone. It is usually dull brown, white or purple. Corundum scores nine on the Mohs scale. It is used to coat the windows of spacecraft and satellites. It is also ground into emery to make sandpaper and nail files.

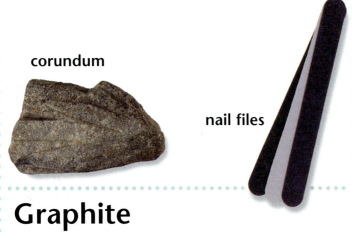

corundum

nail files

# Gypsum

Gypsum is found in many **sedimentary rocks**. It is usually colourless, white, grey, green, yellow, brown or red. Gypsum scores two on the Mohs scale. It is used to make plaster and cement for building.

daisy gypsum

gypsum paving slabs

# Graphite

Graphite is found in slate and schist. It is usually dark grey to black. Graphite is a soft mineral, scoring between one and two on the Mohs scale. It is used in pencils, polishes, batteries and brushes for electric motors.

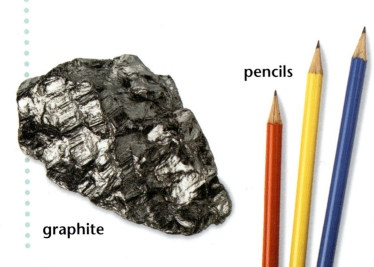

pencils

graphite

# Hematite

Hematite is found in **igneous rocks**. There are several different types of hematite, and each one is a different colour. Hematite scores between five and six on the Mohs scale. It is used to make jewellery or crushed into red powder to colour paint.

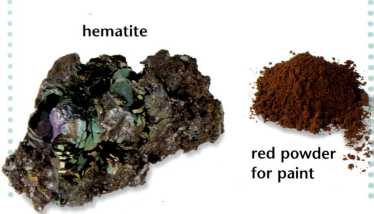

hematite

red powder for paint

# Gemstones

Some **minerals** are very colourful. They are called gemstones and are used to make jewellery.

## Blue agate

There are many different types of blue agate. It is usually blue and purple. It is formed in igneous rock. It is used to make jewellery.

carnelian

lapis lazuli

turquoise

diamond

onyx

blue agate

smoky quartz

Gemstones are used to make jewellery.

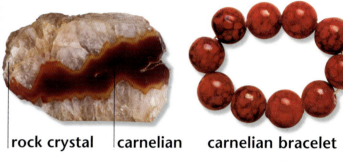

rock crystal | carnelian | carnelian bracelet

## Carnelian

Carnelian is a version of chalcedony. It is red and leaves a white streak if scraped across a tile.

chalcedony

chalcedony bowl

## Chalcedony

Chalcedony is usually frosty grey and white with streaks of quartz. It is used to make bowls, vases and plates.

# Metals

Some **minerals** are **metals**. They include gold, silver, copper, nickel, lead, platinum and titanium. Metals have been important in human history ever since the Stone Age. The discovery of how to work copper, tin and iron led to the use of metal tools.

Metals are found mixed with minerals in **ores**. They are dug up with the ore by mining machines. First the ores are **smelted** or heated until the metal is separated from the ore. Then the metal is taken out and used.

## Properties of Metals

- Metals are excellent conductors of heat and electricity.

- They can be hammered into thin sheets or made into wire.

**wires**

**metal toy robot**

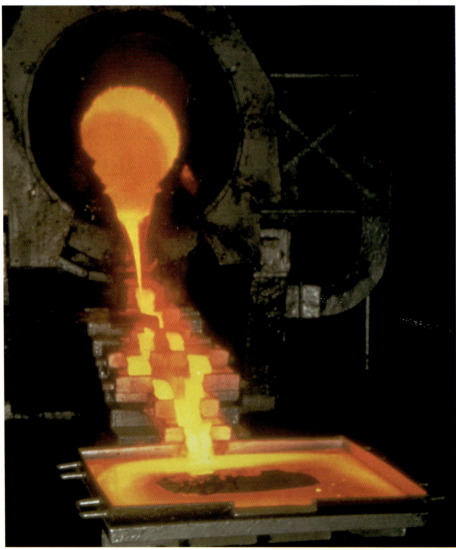

Iron ore is melted in a furnace to separate the pure iron.

# Aluminium

Aluminium is silvery white. It is strong, light and conducts electricity very well. Aluminium is used in aircrafts, buildings, furniture, drinks cans and foil.

aluminium foil

aluminium ore

# Gold

Gold is found in **igneous rock**. It is yellow and easy to shape. Gold is used to make jewellery, fillings for teeth and statues.

gold nugget

This solid gold mask was made for the coffin of a ruler in Ancient Egypt.

# Copper

Copper is reddish brown. It conducts heat and electricity very well. Copper is used to make electrical wires, pipes, saucepans, brass and bronze.

copper pan

copper ore

# Iron

Iron is found with other minerals in iron ore. It is strong, hard and easy to shape. Iron is used to make steel. Steel is one of the world's most useful metals. It is used for many things, including tools and cars.

steel screws

iron ore

# A Rock and Mineral Collection

Now you have been introduced to rocks and **minerals**, you might like to start your own collection. Look out for rocks and minerals in your home, on the ground or at school. When you find a rock or mineral, label it and say where you found it. Then store it in a box with the rest of your collection.

## Collecting Rocks

You can find rocks everywhere. Here are some tips:

• Ask permission to collect rock specimens, or samples, on private property.

• Use a magnifying glass to look at the rocks.

• Use this book to help you identify the specimens.

• Examine specimens under a microscope.

• Patterns in rocks provide clues to their type. The rock's colour and the size of its grains will help you identify what it is made from and how it was formed.

It's easy to start your own rock and mineral collection.

# Glossary

**crust** — rocky outer shell of the Earth

**crystals** — particles in melted rock that form as the rock cools

**fossils** — remains, prints or traces of ancient plants and animals

**grains** — tiny pieces of rock

**igneous rock** — rock formed when magma cools and hardens on the surface or inside the Earth's crust

**lava** — liquid rock or magma that flows onto the Earth's surface

**magma** — liquid rock that exists beneath the Earth's surface

**metal** — shiny material that is a good conductor of heat and electricity

**metamorphic rock** — rock that has been changed by pressure and heat

**minerals** — substances found in the Earth which make up rock

**ores** — minerals from which useful metal can be removed

**sedimentary rock** — layers of rock and other materials that press together and harden

**smelt** — to melt an ore to separate out the metal

# Index

aluminium 29

basalt 8, 10

chalk 15

conglomerate 15

copper 27, 28, 29

corundum 23, 24

crust 4, 7, 11, 12, 19, 22

crystals 8, 9, 22

diamonds 11, 23, 25, 26

feldspar 9, 22, 23

fossils 13

gemstones 25–27

gneiss 5, 18

gold 28, 29

granite 9, 10

graphite 24

gypsum 23, 24

halite 14

hematite 24

hornfels 17, 18

iron 28, 29

kimberlite 11

lava 7, 10

limestone 14–15, 16, 24, 26

magma 7, 9, 10, 19

marble 17, 19

metals 28–29

mica 9, 18

minerals 4, 6, 8, 11, 14, 16, 18, 19, 21, 22–29, 30

Mohs scale 23

obsidian 11

ore 28, 29

quartz 9, 15, 18, 22, 23, 25, 27

quartzite 17, 20

rocks
    igneous 6, 7–11, 24, 25
    metamorphic 6, 17–21, 24
    sedimentary 6, 12–16, 24

sandstone 12, 16, 17

schist 20, 24

shale 16, 17, 24

slate 17, 21, 24

talc 23

volcanoes 7